Affiliate Marketing

A Step By Step Guide On How To Make Money Online With Affiliate Marketing

Dan Moore

The trademarks that are used are without any consent, and the publication of the trademark is without permission or backing by the trademark owner. All trademarks and brands within this book are for clarifying purposes only and are the owned by the owners themselves, not affiliated with this document.

TABLE OF CONTENTS

Page intentionally left blank

The internet has been making more people rich for so many years now than any other business platform on the planet. It is truly extraordinary how easy it is to make money online using affiliate marketing.

The question is, what is affiliate marketing? The answer is: you (called "an affiliate") act as the marketing vehicle for millions of products out there that need buyers. As an affiliate marketer, you are essentially a salesman selling great products that you believe in or have an interest in (you can choose from literally millions of affiliate products), but there are no conventional "sales" jobs involved in selling them.

Generally speaking affiliate programs are marketing programs offered by web advertisers or merchants that recruit website owners and bloggers. The merchants provide banner ads, links and buttons for website owners to place on their website to market the merchant's products. In turn, the website owner or blogger will receive a referral fee or commission when a customer purchases a product that is delivered through an affiliate link.

When you are looking for an affiliate program there are some things you need to consider before choosing which company you are going to take arms with. You can advertise a product or a service.

If you want to become an affiliate it is not that hard. You simply go on the website you choose and look for their affiliate link program. Usually you will be logged in and so you will get a unique affiliate ID along with some banners and links.

You should place these links on your website so that your potential audience can click on those links and, if your potential customer became a lead you will receive a commission. Just because you signed up for an affiliate program does not mean that you are actually going to drive traffic to your website.

You can:

a) drive organic traffic through the people that constantly visit your blog or site.

b) run ads so that you can create a successful Lead Generation.

What do we mean for Lead Generation?

Is the process of attracting prospects or strangers in general into someone interested in your product or service.

Why Lead Generation?

Basically due to the fact that it is easier to sell to a person already interested in one of your product.

First of all you attract the stranger through an ad.

In that ad he or she will find a "call to action" (CTA) like a button or a link that takes the visitor to your landing page.

The "Landing Page" is a page in your website that exchange some value (an ebook, blog post etc...) for the visitor's mail. Once the visitor gives you the email he becomes a lead.

After that, send them to a "thank you page" (a page in which they can see you or read something that thanks them for having shown interest in your blog).

You can create an email list with every email and send to your leads every offer you want.

NB remember to send also articles or video offering them value for free to maintain their interest.

Affiliate marketing networks provide an environment where companies who have something to sell (Advertisers) meet with companies who know how to sell it (Publishers).

Affiliate marketing is all about making money for both parties and often the commissions on sales (buyers you send to the site through your affiliate link) are 50% or higher! Some of the better affiliate programs pay as high as an 80% commission on every sale you make.

Although the product owner handles the product delivery, customer service and virtually everything else beyond your referring targeted potential buyers to them, including overhead, you get paid the same amount if not more as they do on the sale!

If you are running an affiliate marketing business or you are thinking about starting one, please know that it is very important that you invest in an autoresponder from the start. An Internet marketer, (who has been personally involved with affiliate marketing for years), over those years, he has come to realize that a majority of people who visited his site for the first time did not make a purchase. They just left and probably never came back. That meant he had been losing a lot of money and chances are, you are likely fall into the same trap too if you are not well informed.

So he started thinking, what could he do to make sure that he did not lose all of those potential customers who had been coming to his site? That is when he came across autoresponders. I want to say at first he was very adamant about not building a list. But as he grew and continued to learn, he realized that if he truly wanted to turn his affiliate marketing business into a six-figure a year business, he had to start building a list and using an autoresponder. So he did.

He signed up with Aweber, one of the best services out there, created a web form, set up his autoresponder series.

He was surprised to see just how quickly his list and his profits grew. He was attempting to capture the name and email address of everyone who visited his site. He would give them a short report in exchange for their email address. Once they were on his list, he would send out emails once a week giving them tips and information and then telling them about various affiliate products he was promoting. He would pick 4 or 5 different products that complimented his main product and promote them throughout his autoresponder series.

All of the emails that are going out are being sent automatically by his autoresponder. He has set it up to run on autopilot for a full year. That means he can use his time to focus on other things like writing more articles or creating more videos. A very important thing he has learnt during his time online is that the number one reason people will not buy from you is because they do not trust you. Using an autoresponder is the perfect way to help build that trust and turn the browser into a customer for life.

AFFILIATE MARKETING FOR BEGINNERS

The advancements in technology have revolutionized the way things were done in business. Business practices and processes have become more sophisticated and more effective, as they are now backed up by sophisticated equipment and technology. Affiliate marketing is one such marketing practice that has emerged with the various advancements in the internet and has taken the marketing world by storm.

Affiliate marketing results with the collaboration of the merchant who is also the retailer and the affiliate who can be considered as a salesperson. Affiliates can be considered as part of secondary tier of players who are rewarded for bringing in customers for the merchant through their marketing efforts.

Affiliates play a major role in the marketing strategies of the e-businesses. However, they seldom get their deserved share of applause, which is usually contributed to other popular internet marketing methods such as SEO, Pay per click, e-mail marketing, etc. It must always be considered that Affiliate marketing is as effective and as result-oriented as any other marketing method. It is only about the execution strategy.

Affiliate marketing is relatively less complex than other internet marketing methods. Usually, affiliate marketing programs are completely free to join. That way, the merchant can ensure plenty of affiliates working for the business, whereas the affiliates do not have any financial risk involved.

Making money through affiliate marketing is very easy. First, the affiliate can earn throughout the day unlike a traditional business.

Secondly, an affiliate has to promote the website whereas the merchant him or herself handles all the rest of the work such as provision of marketing material, collection of sales money, product shipping and delivery, customer service, etc.

Affiliates can work from home in a flexible manner not having to worry about timings or deadlines. Instead, it is just an easy way of making money on the go. You can do it along with your job for some extra cash or rely completely on it for your earnings. On the other hand, it is a lucrative business for merchants. This is because they get active people to promote their business. It is obviously less expensive than other forms of internet marketing because merchants do not face any continuous

operational costs for their marketing, as in case of internet advertising or banner posting. Instead, affiliates are only paid when a unit of product is sold.

Therefore, there are no heavy fixed costs. A couple of businesses owe their success to affiliate marketing. Amazon.com is one such example, as it relied heavily on affiliate marketing for the promotion of its business. Merchants can run their in-house affiliate programs, or they can also outsource to another intermediary who is responsible for tracking sales referred by affiliates.

Affiliate marketing is indeed one of the most successful and effective methods of internet marketing. However, it must be kept in mind that the effectiveness of affiliate marketing depends heavily on the quality of affiliates you have. Additionally, it is an ongoing process that requires constant maintenance and management.

TYPES OF AFFILIATE MARKETING

What is fascinating about affiliate marketing is that you can earn commissions in more ways than most people think.

Affiliate marketing programs have never been more popular than they are today. For merchants, the appeal of such programs is cost-effective advertising, while affiliates find such programs attractive because they provide a quick and easy way to generate an income. Once considered a sideline, affiliate programs now play a vital role in the world of Internet marketing. There are a limitless number of programs from which affiliates can choose. However, most fall under one of two categories: pay-per-performance (PPP) and pay-per-click (PPC).

- ***Pay-Per-Click***

PPC is the more popular of the two programs for affiliates who are running small businesses. With this program, the affiliate is paid for each visitor that clicks from his or her site to that of the merchant's. The affiliate is paid regardless of whether or not a sale is made. The fee paid for each click is typically nominal and generally does not exceed one dollar.

- ***Pay-Per-Performance***

PPP affiliate marketing is favored by many merchants. This is because a fee is paid only if a sale is made through the efforts of the affiliate. For dedicated affiliate marketers, however, such programs are quite lucrative. This is because the affiliate will earn a commission on each sale, which typically ranges from 15% to 20% of the total cost of the goods or services purchased by the customer. There are two subdivisions of pay-per-performance affiliate programs: pay-per-sales (PPS) and pay-per-lead (PPL).

- ***Pay-Per-Sale***

With pay-per-sale affiliate marketing, the affiliate is paid a specific fee whenever he or she redirects a visitor to the merchant's site and a purchase is made. This predetermined fee will depend on the specific agreement between the affiliate marketer and the merchant. However, such fees are always much higher than the pay-per- click fee mentioned above.

- ***Pay-Per-Lead***

Pay-per-lead affiliate marketing programs are frequently used by finance and insurance companies who heavily rely on leads for company growth. With such programs, affiliates are paid whenever visitors fill out application forms or similar documents, provided they have landed on the merchant's site through the efforts of the affiliate.

• *Unattached Affiliate Marketing*

This type of affiliate marketing will not require too much work from you, you do not even have to set up an affiliate marketing blog like those for Amazon Affiliate Programs. This is more like a PPC marketing (pay-per-click) where you just show affiliate ads on sites that allow this kind of marketing and then get a commission for each click through that web users make on the ads.

• *Related Affiliate Marketing*

This type of marketing is where you are required to have some level of involvement and this is where you create an affiliate marketing blog or website and always show affiliate links on almost all of your website or blog pages. You also earn a commission for each time a web user clicks through the affiliate links.

- *Involved Affiliate Marketing*

This kind of marketing may require you to actually use the products or services before you write a review about them and you should be able to write a more comprehensive and honest reviews.

Affiliate programs is a great way to make residual income. The internet has become more popular than ever before for those who are seeking a steady income, other than a nine to five.

Affiliate programs are the easiest home based business to start and most are completely free to join with no costs to get started. Most offer a website and plenty of advice on how to get started.

Keep in mind, affiliate programs are a way for companies to advertise online by marketing a product or idea and affiliates earn commissions through their efforts. Putting together a marketing strategy is what an affiliate does to promote the product or idea.

There are people earning great sums of money as an affiliate. One thing for sure, it takes hard work, luck and research. What they will not tell you, most, not all of the top earners had a lot of support, in the way of mentors or friends that help guide them to their successful financial state.

If you are like me, starting from the ground, you will be successful, but it is going to take a lot of hard work, research, and patience.

If you are starting from ground zero, you will need a computer with an internet connection. The fact that most people have one, is the why a home based business can be run easily.

Type affiliate programs or home based business opportunities in your browser and visit various websites. If you find one or two that sound interesting, bookmark them and come back later to research the opportunity. Making sure you understand the product, and how you are to make commission as affiliate member. Do not be fooled by all the hype and testimonies. It takes too much work to jump into a program and to find out it is costly and the tools are too hard to understand, they do not work or they are just plain useless. The same goes for e-mail marketing. If you have been contacted through an e-mail promotion that sounds promising, visit the site, contact the person who sent the email and ask questions.

You must understand how the program works, as well as the terms. It is more than building a down line of people; it is also based upon selling real and useful products.

Building an affiliate program will take some time, but they are made to produce residual income and with the right one, you will realize your financial goal

AFFILIATE MARKETING PROGRAMS FOR BEGINNERS

CLICKBANK

ClickBank is the most popular affiliate marketing program for beginners. It is also the biggest marketplace for digital goods.

I prefer digital goods because they have higher profit margins (versus physical goods which have shipping and handling costs + inventory costs). You can literally find digital products in almost any industry.

Here are some examples: arts and entertainment, betting systems, business and investing, E-Business and E-Marketing, education, home and garden, health and fitness, languages, self-help, sports, spirituality, travel and so on and so forth.

You can pick whatever product you want to promote and you get a customized link that tracks back to you when a sale is made (called a "HopLink").ClickBank is they only payout through paychecks.

COMMISSION JUNCTION (CJ)

Commission Junction (CJ) is very similar to ClickBank, except they have physical goods and cost per action options (CPA), too.

CPA is when an advertiser pays you based on a specific action that must be taken, such as filling out a contact request, newsletter sign up, registration, or even making a sale.

Just like ClickBank, they have lots of industries to choose from and it is free to join.

CJ is a little more strict when accepting you as an affiliate (publisher) because you first need to be approved by the advertiser you want to promote for.

In regards to payouts, CJ pays you through checks or direct deposit.No PayPal option.

JVZOO

JVZoo is much like ClickBank.It is all digital goods and they have products from all industries.The differences are that sellers have to approve you before you can promote their products. You also keep more of what you earn whereas with ClickBank, they take a larger portion of your earnings. Lastly, JVZoo does payout through PayPal.

AMAZON ASSOCIATES

Amazon is the biggest online store on the planet. When you signup for their affiliate program, you can promote any product you want (books, headphones, jewelry, tablets, guitars, etc.)

You will be given a unique link, that when someone clicks on and buys, you will earn a commission.

For example, maybe you just bought a new pair of headphones, and you wrote a blog post about how awesome they are.

If you stick your affiliate link in that blog post, you will earn a commission when someone clicks and buys.

But what if they do not buy the headphones? Instead, they get distracted and buy something else?

You still earn a commission for that (which is pretty cool). The bad news about working with Amazon, is the very low commissions, so the money you make really depends on the price of the product you are trying to sell. That is the reason high ticket affiliate programs will be recommended.

Actually, there is another bad news, working with Amazon is amazing because everyone knows the platform, his marketing and his customer service; but keep in mind that is one day Amazon decides to close your account, your career end with it.

> You have to identify a product or service for which there is a need. You could start by searching for "Affiliate Programs" in the Search Engines.

> The product or service should be relevant to your website.

> It is always wise to join an affiliate program that is long standing, safe and secure and has a good reputation in the Internet world. This can be easily verified from the Better Business Bureau or other similar organizations. Visits Forums and Discussion Groups will also provide you with a lot of useful information.

> Most affiliate program providers give a commission of 5% to 50%. The commission you earn for the sale of a product is your main income. So while choosing an affiliate program, you should

study the paid out and decide on a program that pays at least 40% for you to run your business successfully.

➢ There should be a proper tracking system in place to record all the clicks and sales made through the text links and banners placed on your website, e-mails and other advertisements.

➢ An important factor that is often overlooked, is the "click per sale ratio". This indicates the number of clicks that have to be made to a Text Link or Banner to generate a sale. This will give you an idea as to how much traffic is needed before a sale is made.

➢ How often are commissions paid? This is another important matter that should be considered. Most reputed organizations pay their affiliates monthly or when they accumulate a minimum commission of $100 to $ 150 or as indicated by you. You should avoid any program that requires too many sales to reach the minimum amount.

➢ Affiliate Programs are generally single tier or two tiers. A single tier program pays you for whatever business you have generated. On the other hand a two tier program pays you for the business you have generated and also a commission for the sales generated by a sub- affiliate, you have sponsored. A two tier program is always advantageous.

➢ Long standing reputed organizations provide a whole range of tools and resources such as Banners, Text Links, Brochures, Websites and training for their affiliates. When choosing look out for such organizations because they certainly make life much easier and helps you grow your home based business.

➢ Finally, you must read and understand the agreement before you join as an affiliate even if it happens to be the best organization in the world.

If you get an unsolicited email inviting you to join an affiliate network and it is asking for an upfront payment, then you definitely have to scrutinize them and find out whether or not they are scam or legit. Go to the Better Business Bureau (BBB) and find out about the company, if you can not find any, then go to affiliate marketing forums and discussion boards. They would know a lot about these scam sites as news spreads fast in social media and forums. Another thing to look for, is if these people are selling you unrelated products or something that you will never be able to use, like the $350 "Secrets to Affiliate Marketing Success" book or some other catchy titles; although a few are genuine but they do not charge you that high.

The truth is you can learn basic affiliate marketing from top ranking websites and blogs. In fact, they can teach you more useful information than all those specialized books and DVDs that other people are selling. Becoming an affiliate is free when you sign up to affiliate marketing programs and the only thing that will really cost you money is web hosting, which is around $70 - $100 a year for your affiliate marketing blog. A few other expenses may include a unique website or blog logo (optional), hire a blog writer (optional because you can write the blogs yourself) and probably paid advertising to promote your website or blog (optional).

If you are building your business online you know what I am talking about. From not getting enough sleep because you are still doing your day job and worrying about how your going to pay your credit because of the PPC you have put on it, to get your kid up for school in the morning.

1. *Choosing a Profitable Niche* - Choosing a profitable niche is the most important thing you can do in the internet marketing business. You must have a good idea of what you put into a business you will get back ten fold.

I have a quick exercise for choosing a niche that is worth revisiting. Consider your niche carefully. A lot time and energy will be devoted to your future. This may be different from some teachings which will have you starting multiple sites in multiple niches just to "make money online". It is far better to build a profitable business, and to focus on that business exclusively. Always focus on one thing at a time.

Now, more than ever, the niche can shape your life. It can be used to create your lifestyle. Think about the options and opportunities you wish you had. What would you do if money was not an issue?

Most people work hard on research and really get hung up on the numbers. How many searches is enough? What search volume am I looking for exactly? It can get out of control.

2. *Working with Affiliate Links and HTML Code-* The technical side of creating affiliate links, or working with HTML code, is a hurdle for many people. Most merchants make it easy by giving you copy and paste code to work with, but there are times that you want to make changes to that code for a nicer touch. If its hard for you to work with affiliate linking, or if your links are ugly just remember everyone has gone through the same problem. Just keep learning and you will get better results.

You can use sites like Bitly to generate a good looking link

3. *Getting Traffic-* Getting qualified traffic. Traffic alone is not enough. You definitely want good traffic. The visitors must be targeted, and you have a strong message to match the offer to your guest. The most obvious source of traffic is search engines. You want to be right there, front and center, when the market is searching for what you are offering. When it comes to traffic, remember quality beats quantity. Target your market as much as you possibly can. This will often result in fewer unique visitors, but higher conversion rates - and means higher sales and more money on the end game.

Blogging is one of the best ways to get in front of your target market. Publish content off-site in other places such as article directories, squidoo, hub spot, wikis, etc. Niche communities are a great place to find your market as well, and include: forums, discussion groups, and Facebook groups. In all of these cases, including Social Media, your goal is to become known and provide value to the conversation in your market.

4. *Making Sales* - A lack of commissions boils down to one of two problems: traffic or conversions. Make sure you know which of the two is the actual issue, and work from there. When people say they are having trouble making sales the real issue is lack of traffic, or poor targeting. You need 1,000 visitors to an offer to determine the true conversion rate. If you have less than that, or your traffic is less than targeted, go back to work on traffic first.

It is important to consider the intent of the search with each keyword phrase, and deliver exactly what they are searching for. You do not want to serve information to someone who is not ready to make a purchase, do not try to sell products to someone who is not looking for that product or service. Use keyword phrases to make sales.

5. *Your Script-* Writing content is an issue for a lot of people. It helps to look at it from another angle, rather than just a crappy task you have to perform consider it part of the conversation. You start by choosing a keyword phrase to target or write about, and then you sit there with a blank screen and try to come up with an article or a blog post for that topic. Try to imagine someone looking for an answer to their question on the other end of their computer.

IS AFFILIATE MARKETING RIGHT FOR MY BUSINESS?

Affiliate marketing is one of the most powerful and effective means of gaining new customers, regardless of your product or service. Affiliate marketing exposes your business to new customers and can get you out of your marketing rut. Additionally, when you initiate an affiliate marketing campaign, you are in control. You determine the commission rate you pay and pay only when your affiliates make a sale. It is a no loss operation for you because you only pay when a sale is made.

WHAT ARE THE STARTUP COSTS?

When you start an affiliate program you have the choice of handling the operations yourself or having it managed by an affiliate network. The costs for either choice are reasonable and generally start around a some hundred dollars. Additionally, as a business owner do not forget that many of your costs may be tax deductible. To start an affiliate marketing program in house, costs will include:

i. Affiliate management software.

ii.Affiliate marketing support including a website that answers affiliate questions and a means for them to contact you if any issues arise.

Iii.Affiliate marketing materials including banner ads, copy, coupons, and promotional content.

iv.An affiliate marketing contract agreement.

v.Tracking software to track cookies, click throughs, payments, etc.

If you choose to hire an affiliate network to handle your program they generally charge a flat fee or a percentage of what you pay out each month.

HOW MUCH TIME WILL IT TAKE OUT OF MY WORKDAY OR WORKWEEK?

Most experts agree that it will take you about an hour and a half each day to manage your affiliate program. They also recommend you to budget more time in the first few months of your program, approximately three to three and half hours a day. Even the most efficient affiliate managers spend about 50 minutes a day managing their affiliate program.

Professional affiliate managers generally spend an average of 30-70 hours a month dedicated to managing, tracking and promoting your affiliate program.

SHOULD I USE AN AFFILIATE NETWORK?

Do you have an extra 2 hours a day for the next two or three months? Do you have an hour a day to devote to managing your program after the initial three month program is complete? An affiliate network, while it may be a bit more expensive on the outset, can help you focus your time on other profit generating tasks. Additionally, an affiliate network can help expose your affiliate program to a wide variety of experience affiliates, which means more money in your bottom line and more exposure overall.

That being said, there are a tremendous number of effective in-house solutions including some you are likely already familiar with like 1shoppingcart.com and affiliatepro.com. These programs will help you stay 100% in control of your affiliate program and are effective at managing your program.

HOW SHOULD I PAY AFFILIATES? WHAT TYPE OF COMMISSION WORKS BEST?

This is a very important decision because it not only affects your profits, the right commission rate will help you recruit top-notch affiliates. The general rule of thumb is to set your default commission rate at a rate you can afford to pay while leaving room for time limited commission increase offers, promotions, and private offers. For example, if you can afford to pay 50% of your gross profit margin, pay 25% instead and tier it so that after a sales goal is reached they earn 30% or you can bump it up to 50% during the holidays or during typically low sales times.

HOW DO I RECRUIT AFFILIATES?

Your customers may be your best affiliates. After all, they already appreciate and enjoy your products or services. A simple link on your website is a good place to start. Here are a few ways to find quality affiliates:

i.Online forums. These are excellent places to meet and greet and connect with like minded individuals. They are also a good resource for affiliates who are interested in, motivated, and qualified to sell your products and services. Using a forum, you can announce your affiliate program. Be careful to not 'sell' on the forum as most forums look down on this and may kick you off. Additionally, you can include a link to your affiliate site in your signature.

Ii.Find websites that link to your competitors and approach them about being an affiliate for you. Likewise, you can find affiliates using your favorite search engine and contact them about joining your program.

One last way is to join an affiliate network or become listed on an affiliate directory. This will ensure that affiliate marketers who are searching for new products and services to promote. However, keep in mind that many beginner marketers also seek products and services to promote through affiliate directories and they may lose interest and motivation before they ever make a sale. This is not a strong deterrent because they do not get paid unless they make a sale, however it should be noted.

WHAT IS THE BEST WAY TO COMMUNICATE WITH MY AFFILIATES?

Email is the general tool of choice, which makes an auto responder a fantastic tool for basic emails like the welcome email, introducing promotions, coupons, sending links and banner ads, and answering Frequently Asked Questions**(FAQ).** It is also generally advisable to have an email address, fax number, and telephone number available for when affiliates have questions that are not answered by your frequently asked questions web page or when they simply want to speak with you.

- ### *How Do I Motivate Affiliates?*

Money motivates no doubt about it. That being said, affiliates are also motivated by feeling that they are important to you. This means when they ask for your time, you give it. Additionally, promotions, bonuses, prizes, contests, and commission increases are all tools to motivate and inspire affiliates. Constant communication will also help remind your affiliates that you are out there and invested in their success.

- ### *Do I Need To Hire An Affiliate Manager?*

The answer to this question really depends on your needs. How large is your company? Do you have the time to manage your program? Do you have the skills to manage your program? An affiliate manager is the person that:

Recruits affiliates

Communicates with affiliates

Develops, tracks, and reports on promotions

Develops programs to enhance affiliate program

Motivates affiliates

Tracks sales and pays affiliates

Monitors your competition

These are all extremely important functions and if you have the time to handle them yourself, excellent! If you do not, then consider hiring an affiliate manager.

- ***How Do I Find Or Hire An Affiliate Manager?***

Outsourcing an affiliate manager is fairly easy to do. There are hundreds available with a quick online search. You can ask associates,inquire at online forums, or post an advertisement seeking someone to fill the position. Depending on the complexity of your affiliate program, you could consider a well qualified virtual assistant for the job. The skills your affiliate manager will need are:

Organizational skills

Communication skills

Attention to detail

Knowledge of online business, internet marketing, and basic ecommerce operations

Basic html and graphic experience are a plus because they are going to be representing you, you will want to make sure they are personable.

Affiliate marketing is considered one of the best ways to earn money online. I know that you must have heard or read a lot of stories about people that are making mega money online selling other peoples product and you want some of that cash for yourself.

As you will agree with me, Affiliate marketing has evolved into a very popular online business opportunity where a person (you) earns a commission by recommending "other people's product" to buyers, or by helping to generating leads (customers) to an online merchant.

It is a very good business but a lot of affiliate programs look like a lot of work for not all that much gain. But not all of them, I am happy to say. This is where you must do your research before venturing into any affiliate program to get the best affiliate sites that will make you money and not just make you work for nothing. So what should you look for before signing up to one of them?

Here are the three steps you must take before you sign up an as affiliate

- ***Affiliate Site Review***

The first thing to do is check out the top affiliate review sites and find out which affiliate sites are the best. There are many different affiliate programs to choose from and the affiliate review sites will discuss what separates the best affiliate sites from the rest.

- ***Compare The Reviewed Sites***

After completing the sites review exercise, take the top five or top ten programs and check each one. Ensure you spend time reading the reviews of every of the top five to top ten program comparing them with each other. Pick at least two among the five or ten you ended up with.

- **Success Stories**

Finally, after comparing and picking your top two affiliate site or product. Search for success stories related to those two programs you have chosen. If there are a lot, you may just have found the program you need. Having two trusted affiliate programs will help you earn money faster.

The affiliate agreement created by the merchant and agreed by the affiliate, defines all aspects of the affiliate program and typically includes:

- Types of Web sites merchant will accept into the affiliate program
- Types of links allowed and guidelines regarding their use.
- Schedule and payments terms of fees and commissions
- Terms of usage of merchant logo, name and web content
- Technical specification that your web site must meet, if any
- Restrictions on types of content that may appear on affiliate sites
- Requirements for compliance with all government laws, ordinances, rules, and regulations.

WHY AFFILIATE MARKETING IS PROFITABLE FOR E-BUSINESS

If you have been considering an affiliate marketing venture, there are some very good reasons why you should go with this method of generating steady incomes.

1.One of the first advantages of affiliate marketing for the new entrepreneur is that the startup cost is very low. Most companies that offer affiliate marketing programs do not require any type of monetary investment on the part of the affiliate.

2.The second expenses are limited to what you have to pay to connect with the Internet, the software you may need to load on your computer, and a web site where the ads associated with the affiliate marketing program can be placed. With web site hosting such an inexpensive service these days, setting up your own web site for the affiliate ads will be a breeze.

3. Another reason that affiliate marketing is such a moneymaker is the fact that there are so many different types of ways to set up the program. You can go with the pay per click option, which works out great when it comes to promoting special offers. Ads that lead to product review sites often are a way to allow product users to go through your portal and leave comments on the items they purchase.

SOME AFFILIATE MARKETING MISTAKES ONE MUST AVOID

While affiliate marketing is a great way to earn a living, the fact is that many people become discouraged and drop out of programs. In many instances, the failure to be successful with affiliate marketing has to do with making a few simple mistakes.

Here are some examples of those mistakes and why they should be avoided.

1.A low-quality website with no original content and tossing in some affiliate links. While it is certainly true that you need to have a web site up and running in order to participate in an affiliate program, there is also the need to apply some effort forgetting the word out about your site. Otherwise, the chances of people visiting your web site and clicking on one of the links are pretty slim.

2.Another mistake many affiliate partners make is not choosing products that have some relevance to the content of your web site.

3.Keeping your site content and the ads more or less relevant to one another will make it easier to generate revenue, and not fail as an affiliate marketer. Now, this may seem intuitive but many make this mistake in subtle ways (i.e. they mismatch their customers with products).

4.One final mistake that many affiliate marketers make is not sprucing up their web sites from time to time. Keeping the content fresh is one way of building and keeping a loyal reading audience because keeping the same old look and the same old text with nothing new to entice people back is a sure way to limit your chances at being a successful affiliate marketer. The fact is that you do have to proactively promote your site, keep the content fresh, and make sure the ads have some connection to the subject matter of your site.

SOME IMPORTANT BENEFITS OF AFFILIATE MARKETING

1. COMMISSION BASIS

For affiliate marketers this is a key advantage as every time that somebody makes a purchase, the affiliate receives a set commission of the profit.

For affiliate merchants this is an advantage as they only pay the marketer when they make a sale, so no money is wasted on marketing spend.

2. HUGE AUDIENCE

For affiliate marketers - having built up various marketing lists or websites, they can make use of their huge audience base and ensure that the traffic they send over to the merchant is qualified and that sales are made, making the affiliate more money.

For affiliate merchants - they receive access to a wider audience base than they may have had before, creating more interest in their products, resulting in more sales and all without investing any more money or time.

3. EASE

For affiliate marketers - once they have set up their additional sites and links across to the merchant, it is very simple to manage and often affiliates will continue to make money from sales without having done anything for months.

For affiliate merchants - they do not have to invest time and money writing content or creating expensive images in order to promote their services or products.

Instead affiliates will apply to be a part of their programme and all the merchant need do is have many affiliates all working towards promoting their products or services and wait for the sales to flood in.

4. STEADY COST

For affiliate marketers - building on the last point, an affiliate can keep receiving commission from sales of a product or service for years, despite not doing a lot of work to promote it. You do need to invest time at the start but then you have a regular source of income coming in for the market life of the service or product.

For affiliate merchants - they set up all the costs so the chance to make a huge profit on sales without having spent much on marketing, is very likely. They do not have to pay their affiliates much per sale to make the business relationship worthwhile, as it tends to work best on a quantity basis so everyone is happy with the set amounts.

5. BRAND VISIBILITY

For affiliates - there is a lot to be gained reputation wise from working with a range of brands and you will find that you get a lot more work should you be able to prove that you have succeeded with others in the past.

For affiliate merchants - they receive free brand exposure on a continual basis, which is never a bad thing. If you have many affiliates working on promoting your brand, you will soon see a boost in search engine rankings and online sales; Amazon.com is an excellent example of where this has worked in the past.

6. OUTSOURCED EXPERTISE

For affiliate marketers - they get the continued experience to improve and work on their methods of online marketing, investing only their time, not money.

For affiliate merchants - they will be able to use all kinds of affiliates who are experts in SEM (search engine marketing) and SEO (search engine optimisation) without investing a lot of money, yet still manage to get to the top of Google rankings.

7. TRANSPARENCY

For affiliate marketers - through the various affiliate programmes, it is possible to see exactly when sales are made and payment is automatic, so you do not have to worry about chasing merchants for payments.

For affiliate merchants - they can see and manage their R.O.I (return on investment) extremely easily and do not have to worry about tracking the origin of each sale.

8. ONLINE MARKET

For the affiliate marketer - there are an endless number of affiliate programs out there and the demand for online shopping is not going to decrease, so the earning potential for affiliates is huge. You can access any number of markets with your affiliate work, whether you choose jewellery, hygiene, pet insurance or food.

Use long tail pro to find targeted long tail keywords with low competition, ensuring maximum affiliate sale for you.

For the affiliate merchant - as previously mentioned, online demand is not going away any time soon, therefore merchants are able to continue to expand product ranges to meet a range of online markets with the knowledge that they have a number of affiliates on hand to promote quickly and at a low cost.

9. HOME-BASED WORK (AIMED AT AFFILIATE MARKETER)

If you become successful in the world of affiliate marketing then it is entirely possible to create a long term Passive Income from it and a huge bonus to this is that you can work cheaply from home and be your own boss. You do not have to pay to sign up to affiliate programmes and there are a huge number to choose from, all from the comfort of your own home.

10. OVERCOMING TRADITION (AIMED AT AFFILIATE MERCHANT)

Using affiliates to promote your products and services will guarantee that you receive a lot more exposure than you would by using more pricey traditional marketing methods. Having a number of affiliates promoting what you are selling and only being paid when a sale is made, is one of the most cost effective marketing methods ever as well as being incredibly successful.

AFFILIATE MARKETING- CREATE A STREAM OF INCOME!

Obviously, running multiple streams of affiliate marketing income is totally a great idea due to grow your affiliate commission and online business. With those multiple sources of affiliate marketing income, you are running multiple affiliate marketing strategies at the same time. In this book, you will discover and learn some basic steps to run multiple streams of affiliate marketing income.

With those steps, it will be easier for you to run your own affiliate marketing business and build your own multiple streams of affiliate marketing income. You will leverage those simple steps and learn how to maximize your affiliate commission below.

DISCOVER HIGH PERFORMANCE KEYWORDS.

The first step is to discover high performance keywords for your affiliate marketing business. With those keywords, you will ensure yourself to maximize your profits online and earn huge affiliate commission. To discover the high performance keywords, you can use pay per click (PPC) search engine to test and find out which keywords are super-profitable for your business. Without testing systematically, it is difficult to identify which keywords are super-profitable and valuable for your home based affiliate marketing business.

WRITE QUALITY CONTENTS WITH HIGH PERFORMANCE KEYWORDS.

The next step for running multiple streams of affiliate marketing income is to write quality content with those keywords. My recommendation is to focus on your reader's mind.

BUILD YOUR WEBSITE RANKING, BASED ON YOUR CONTENT.

The next step is to upload your content given from previous step on your website. You have to optimize your web page with those high performance keywords as well. It means you must include those high performance keywords into your web page and content for your affiliate website. Also, there are many search engine optimization techniques on the internet to help you to build your website ranking in search engines.

CONSOLIDATE YOUR CONTENT INTO YOUR OWN ARTICLE.

The article marketing is one of the most effective affiliate marketing strategies to drive quality relevancy traffic to your affiliate website. All you have to do is to consolidate your content into the articles. You have to focus on writing, article layout, article structure and article formats. With those stuffs, it is easier for you to maximize the profits through your articles. Additionally, submitting your articles to other article directories is a good idea to build up your reputation and creditability. Also, it will help you drive more quality traffic to your affiliate website.

POST YOUR ARTICLES INTO YOUR BLOG.

To run multiple streams if income, building your own blog with those same articles from the previous step is a great idea. However, you have to customize those articles for your own blog. There is a different between post messages in blogs and articles. You have to use your personality and be more personalised into your blog. For blogging online, you have to build up the relationship with your readers. That is why you have to be more personalised and socialised, rather than writing the articles.

INCLUDE YOUR ARTICLES INTO YOUR NEWSLETTER.

Providing newsletter strategies has proven that it is very powerful to drive more traffic to your affiliate website. Thus, to run multiple streams of affiliate marketing income, newsletter is one of the best strategies you should not forget. You can include your articles from the above step into your newsletter.

PARTICIPANT IN FORUM THROUGH YOUR ARTICLES.

Many studies reveal that participating in forums through your articles will help you skyrocket affiliate commission and grow your affiliate marketing business.

The highest recommendation is to use this strategy properly, rather than trying to sell your affiliate products in the community. You have to share and exchange the ideas and information related to your affiliate products among other people in the forums. That is the best way to maximize the power of forums and articles together!

ADS.

The last step is to run ads properly. With the content and the right keywords from from the previous steps, you can conduct your own online classified ads. The best approach to maximize your profits is to run ads using the same keywords included in your blog.

In this book, you have learnt how to combine several affiliate marketing strategies, like pay per click online advertising, search engine optimization, article marketing, blogging online marketing and email marketing, to run multiple streams of affiliate marketing income. The real key to your success is your *creativity*. You have to combine those affiliate marketing strategies together to maximize your profits.

Most people have heard about affiliate marketing, even if they have not actually started doing it. Affiliate marketing is basically referring people to various products and services around the internet. For each sale you generate through your affiliate link, you earn a commission. The size of the commission depends on the products themselves, who is selling them and the percentage offered by the seller to the affiliate.

But what is actually involved in affiliate marketing? What do affiliates do on a daily basis? How do they earn money and how do they learn what to do?

1 HOW CAN I GET STARTED AS AN AFFILIATE?

Affiliate marketing is huge. There are thousands of people already making their main source of income from the internet. To get started as an affiliate you need to learn some basic strategies and build various methods to generate traffic from the internet to those offers. A lot of affiliates start with a simple blog. Many travelers 'blog' about their travels. If you do not have a passion or interest to blog about, you can start by following an online course which will help.

2 HOW LONG DOES IT TAKE TO MAKE A LIVING?

Some people go into affiliate marketing to create a second income. Some people want to make big money. Depending on how much time you can dedicate to your affiliate business, and how dedicated you are to it, is a big factor in determining your results.

Results vary from person to person. With a large advertising budget and the right business model, some affiliates have replaced their living in 6-12 months. For others it can take years...

Depending on your approach, advertising budget, and business model, it can take between

3 months and several years to build it to a point where it can replace an existing income.

3 CAN ANYONE DO IT?

One of the great things about affiliate marketing is that the technology is now available to allow anyone to build their own online business. As long as you are prepared to learn and implement that knowledge, anyone who can write and send an email, can use online platforms and tools to build their own online business. The main thing you need is the desire to learn. Affiliate marketing is not for everyone though. It does take a lot of hard work and it can take years before you are rewarded financially.

4 WHAT ARE THE PITFALLS OF AN AFFILIATE BUSINESS?

You need to dedicate some time to your affiliate business for it to work for the long term. Some people go into affiliate marketing thinking it is some magic pill which will pay them instantly in cash. Much like a job you can not expect to get out more than you put in. Affiliate marketing is performance related. This means you do not get paid unless you can successfully sell products and services online. If you do not know what you are doing it can take years to do this. You can not be a dabbler and expect to earn the big money. The big earnings are created over years of hard work. Do not expect to achieve this with only a small amount of input.

5 WHAT ARE THE BEST THINGS ABOUT AFFILIATE MARKETING?

Affiliate marketing offers an incredible amount of flexibility and freedom. You can work an affiliate business from anywhere in the world providing you have a laptop and an internet connection. You can choose your own hours and build it up around existing work. Many people come into affiliate marketing because it offers this kind of flexibility. They can choose their priorities in life: spend more time with family, choose your working hours, travel and work abroad. No more commuting to work or working long hours for a boss you do not like.

Affiliate marketing also offers incredible scalability. A business which is local is always limited to the people who can travel to that business. An online business can be global. Using digital products in conjunction with a global reach, you can scale using tools and software to reach thousands of people through digital technology. By using automation much of the work involved with an online business can be pre-built. By building automation into the business model, you can focus your activities on reaching a larger audience through content creation and paid advertising.

6 WHY AM I STRUGGLING WITH MY AFFILIATE BUSINESS?

A lot of people struggle with their affiliate businesses. This can be for a number of reasons. Firstly building up an affiliate business takes time. You need to dedicate a lot of time to an affiliate business in the first place. Only when you reach a 'tipping point' do you really start to see your progress. Many affiliates simply do not realise how much work is involved. They underestimate how much time they need to dedicate to their online business to make it work.

Paid advertising can allow you to grow your affiliate business quickly. But it costs money and you need the right products too. You can not advertise small value items with paid advertising. You will not generate enough profit to cover your advertising costs. You need a range of products and an email list to advertise through.

Content marketing takes much longer to work, depending on your chosen area of business. If you find an untapped niche to market your blog in, you can make some fast progress. However, with a competitive niche you will struggle to get noticed above all the other content which you will have to compete with. There are several reasons why you might struggle. The main one is lack of knowledge. Get the right education first and your affiliate business will move much faster.

7 WHAT IS THE BEST AFFILIATE MODEL TO USE?

There are many different affiliate models, all offering something different to suit the individual. Some affiliates target search traffic and aim to get their content found on Google. Some create their own products and sell them directly to customers. However, having a range of products which you can sell over and over to existing customers is a great model for a long term success. Selling a single item online is limited. It means you can only make one commission from each sale. By choosing membership products to promote which also offer back end sales and a built in sales team, you can benefit from monthly commissions and up-sell commissions for the lifetime of any given customer. Selling membership products is definitely a game changer when it comes to affiliate marketing because you make an income from each customer, rather than a single commission. But a good model to choose is one in which you have a passion for and can keep doing for the long term. Choosing products which you have no interest in is a short sighted plan. Think about what you would like to do online to generate an income. If you choose to go with your passion, your business will last much longer, and be more successful.

8 CAN I JUST SELL MY OWN PRODUCTS?

Many affiliates create their own products to sell online. However, when you are starting out it is a good idea to learn the basics of marketing first. That way you can start earning more quickly from your affiliate business.

I spent a long time creating my own products when I first discovered affiliate marketing. But I did not sell anything because of a couple of reasons.

Firstly I did not research whether my products would have a big enough demand. Secondly I did not know how to market them. By joining a program which teaches you how to market products first, you can start making money more quickly. Do not waste time creating products if you do not know how to sell them. Marketing is a much more important skill for making money online. Once you know this skill, you can then apply it later when marketing your own products and services taking the 100% commissions. Also your own products will be limited in range. By using an existing product range, you can benefit from products which are already selling. You can choose a program which offers high ticket commission, monthly memberships, back end sales and a built in sales team. Building your own products which offers all of these things not a possibility for most people when starting out.

9 WHAT IS THE POINT OF AFFILIATE MARKETING?

Some people struggle with the concept of affiliate marketing. They think it sounds too 'salesy'. When I understood affiliate marketing I immediately found it appealing simply because I needed a flexible way to work around my contract work. I had to drop what I was doing at a moments notice if the phone went. This meant other jobs were awkward to juggle around. No-one wants to employ a 'flaky' employee. I wanted to work from my laptop and affiliate marketing gave me that opportunity. For many people this is the reason why they choose affiliate marketing. They can earn an income from their laptop, choose their working hours and not have a boss or place of employment. You do not have to sell directly to anyone or even talk to a customer. There is no stock to hold. Added to this, the scalability of affiliate marketing which lets you scale up to a global audience and deliver products on autopilot, makes it the best flexible business of the future.

STEPS TO BECOME AN AFFILIATE MARKETER

1. Decide what niche topic you want to use for your blog or website. It is better to write reviews or general information about products or services that you are passionate about, because you will write better articles for them compared to those that you do not like. For instance, if you are mad about crochet or kids bicycles, then that is the niche you should pick for your blog! Affiliate programs have a huge inventory of items for sale and they do include crochets and bicycles for a fact. If you are more of the business-minded individual and you think you can write just about on anything, then by all means pick the niche that is most profitable among the lot.

2. Create your website and purchase a cheap but reliable web hosting. You do not need a web designer to build a website or a blog. You can use WordPress, Weebly, Web.com, Blogger, eHost and others to do that. Using their user-friendly "click and drag" features you can create your blog or website in 5 - 10 minutes!

3. Learn basic SEO and use it on your blog or website. Search engine optimization or SEO is a very good marketing strategy to allow your website to be known throughout the entire internet or at least the majority of it. If your website is easier to find in search engines, then it is more convenient for people to visit it,and more visitors means more money for you.

4. Learn social media marketing to extend your presence online. In reality social media marketing or SMM is also a part of the grand scheme of SEO and without it, your SEO campaign would not be as successful as you had expect it to be. There are literally billions of people hanging around the web on a daily basis and much of them are in social media sites. It would be a logical choice to get visitors there for your website and increase your income potential.

5. Learn about paid advertising and consider it deeply on whether you need to use it or not. Paid ads help because they target the right kind of people who are already looking for products that you promote. Meaning there is a good chance that they will buy. Would not you want them to buy products through your affiliate links? I would!

6. Start filling up your website with content. In case you plan to write boring and unimpressive blogs and articles, then I would advise you to no longer continue in your pursuit of creating an affiliate marketing blog, I promise you people will not want to read your blogs or visit your site. Write articles that will impress you first. This will let you know whether or not people will want to read about what you have to say. If you can find an extremely critical person to judge your writing, then that would be better as it will help you greatly improve on your writing style. Reader engagement is absolute in affiliate marketing. It will determine your income capacity, so do your best in writing content for your site above all else.

REASONS WHY YOU MUST BE AN AFFILIATE MARKETER

An affiliate marketer is someone who gets paid to direct customers or traffic to another service. For example many blogs have affiliate marketing set up to direct customers towards products related to their blog. Many people consider affiliate marketing to be a nice job, here are the top reasons why you must be an affiliate marketer:

- *You Are Your Boss*

The only person stopping you from becoming a wealthy affiliate is yourself. You set your own schedule for marketing and choose what you do. No longer will you have someone yelling at you and telling you what to do.

- ***Let The Income Flow In***

In a "normal" job you are paid by the hour and limited to how much you can work, with affiliate marketing that is different. Internet marketing can be used as many times as you want. You do not have to sign up for just one affiliate marketplace either.

- ***Vacation on Your Time***

A lot of people have to apply to get vacation, when you are an affiliate you get to pick and choose when you go on vacation. You can even bring your work with you if you choose to take a working vacation and earn money while enjoying yourself.

- ***Expanding Market***

Right now online marketing is really taking off because people want to find a way to supplement their income or a whole new way to work. More and more websites are also starting to offer affiliate marketing.

- ***No Expensive Support Structure***

With affiliate marketing the support structure that most businesses require is not needed. The company you are an affiliate for already has its own customer support and other support staff. This will save you a lot of time and money as you will not need to build this infrastructure.

- ***Hands Off Collection***

Almost all affiliate marketing programs handle all of the sales for you. Your website or blog is just a portal to your partner's store. You do not have to worry about accepting payments, shipping products, or any of the time consuming parts of running a business.

- *Working When You Are Not There*

Since affiliate marketing is essentially directing traffic from your website to another website you earn money whether sitting in front of the computer or sleeping in bed. There is a significant amount of time that goes into starting an affiliate marketing program though, you have to set up a website, sign up for a program, and entice people to want follow your links. The more websites that you have set up the more money your program is making you while you are not there. It is like printing money on autopilot.

- ***Do Not Have A Lot Of Money To Start?***

Affiliate marketing is not an expensive area to start delve into. Mainly all you need to do is spend money for hosting and registering a domain. As your money starts to come in you can host multiple domains. There is no need for a physical office or large support staff so a basic affiliate marketing website can be set up with only about $40-50 a year.

- ***The Internet Is Not So Large***

Okay, the internet is actually huge but most people do not go to websites using the URLs any more. The vast majority of people use a search engine to find websites that contain what they are looking for. Fortunately, just a few but powerhouse search engines are required to propel your internet marketing endeavours to new heights. All you need to do to start earning money quickly is get a good placing on a search engine. Some affiliate market places will pay up to $500 per customer referred, depending on the industry.

- ***There Is No Limit***

Most affiliate networks do not place limits on how much money you can earn. Despite the fact that they are paying you, they are still making money. Even if your first program has set a limit, you can easily overcome that by starting with a second program. To maximize your income, pick areas that you can provide additional content to or revolutionize somehow, thereby preparing the ground to becoming a top affiliate.To earn even more money, consider posting links on social media and advertising websites if the programs you choose allow it. These will allow you to have exposure to an even larger number of people.

- ***Many Sources***

There are many different companies that allow you to sign up for an affiliate program. Chances are there is a program in a niche that you are interested or knowledgeable in. Quite often new programs come up.

What are you waiting for? There is a whole world of marketing that is waiting for you to reach out and seize it. Sign up for your first affiliate program today and set up a killer website to start attracting business and earning money.

WHY SO MANY PEOPLE CRASH IN AFFILIATE MARKETING

More and more people are lured into affiliate marketing and you might be one of them. Indeed, affiliate marketing is one of the most effective means of generating a full-time income through the Internet. It is a fair deal between the merchandiser and his affiliates as both benefit from each sale materialized.

Like in other kinds of business, a great deal of the profits in affiliate marketing depends on the affiliates selling, advertising and promoting strategies. Everyday, as affiliate marketing industry expands, competition heightens as well so an affiliate marketer must be creative enough to employ effective and unique ways to convince potential buyers to purchase or avail of the products and services offered. Compared to traditional advertising practices, affiliate programs are more effective, risk-free and cost-efficient.

Reasons People Fail In Affiliate Marketing

So why do many people still fail in affiliate marketing? There are a lot of reasons and a lot of areas in the program to look into.

The most critical aspect in the affiliate program is advertising. It is the most important thing all other kinds of business as well; many affiliate marketers fail in this aspect because they lack hard work. Although it pays be lucky, you cannot merely rely on it. Affiliate marketing is not as simple as directing customers to the business site.

You Must Invest In Yourself

If you want to earn big, of course, you have to invest time and great amount of hard work in promoting the products. The competition is very high and customers nowadays are very wise, too, as earlier mentioned. After all, who does not want to get the best purchase? That is, to pay less and get more in terms of quality and quantity.

Being Prepared Is Critical In Affiliate Marketing

Lack of preparation is also a reason why one fails in affiliate marketing, whether he is a merchandiser or an affiliate. Part of the preparation is researching. On the part of the merchant, he has to be highly selective in choosing the right affiliate websites for his affiliate program.

In order to be sure he has the best choices, he must have exhausted his means in looking for highly interested affiliates whose sites are sure fit to his products and services.

The affiliate site's visitors must match his targeted customers. On the other hand, the affiliate marketer must likewise research on the good-paying merchandisers before he signs up for an affiliate program.

He must ensure that the merchant's products and services match his interests so he can give his full dedication and attention to the program.

He can get valuable information by joining affiliate forums, comparing different affiliate programs and reading articles on affiliate marketing where he can get tips from experienced affiliate marketers on how to choose the best merchants and products with high conversion rate.

Your Website Is Critical To The Success Of Your Affiliate Business

The website is a very important tool in the whole affiliate program. You should plan how your site is going to be, from domain name to the design, the lay-out, the content, ads and marketing.

Some users are particular about what they see at first glance and thus when they find your site ugly, they will not spend their time looking at your site. On the other hand, there are those who want information more than anything else. Marketers with "rich-content" web sites are usually the ones who prosper in this business because the content improves traffic to the site.

Websites with high quality contents and relevant keywords are the best optimized sites. Having the right information about the product and service and not just a bunch of empty hyped-up advertisements will allow you to earn big in affiliate marketing even when you are asleep.

If you are not able to sustain the interest of your site visitor, you will not be able to lead them to purchase. No click-through means no sale and thus, no income on your part.

Selecting a top level domain name is also crucial to the success of the affiliate program. Lots of affiliate sites do not appear in the search engine results because they are deemed by affiliate managers as personal sites.

Major search directories and engines would think of your site as a transient one and thus, they will not list it in the directory.

Know first what you are going to promote, before you decide on the domain name. Even if they feature the exact products the customer is looking for, the customer might think the site is not relevant and becomes weary of the site contents.

An Educated Affiliate Is A Successful Affiliate

Above all, an affiliate marketer must be willing to learn more. Certainly, there are still a lot of things to learn so an affiliate marketer must continue to educate himself so he can improve his marketing strategies. Many fail because they do not grow in the business and they are merely concerned about earning big commissions quickly.

If you want long-term and highly satisfactory results, take time to learn the ins and outs of the business. Continue to improve your knowledge especially with the basics in marketing ranging from advertising to programming, web page development, and search engine optimization techniques.

Likewise, study the needs and wants of your site users and how different merchandisers compete with each other.

If your initial attempts are failures do not give up. Keep plugging away. Do not get disappointed. You see, thousands are attracted by money and the fact one can skyrocket incomes through affiliate marketing and so they sign up in any affiliate program without carefully understanding every aspect of the business.

When they do not get instant results, they quit and sign up for another program and repeat the process of just copying links and referring them to others. When you sign up for an affiliate program, do not expect to get rich in an instant.

Work on your advertising strategies and be patient. Stay focused and become the best student you can be and you will not be one that crashes in affiliate marketing.

HOW TO GET YOUR AFFILIATE LINK ONLINE AND HOW TO PROMOTE IT

The beauty of affiliate marketing is that unlike a salesman in the real world, you are not trying to convince anyone of anything. You just register a domain (which is recommended but not required) and put up a product review minisite, a one page website that describes and promotes all the features and benefits of the product being promoted.

Although a product review site is recommended for the best results, it does require that you do have some web space on the Internet. Hosting accounts are available for just a few dollars a month so this should be within anyone's reach that has a true desire to be an affiliate. Many review sites can be placed on one hosting account. In fact you could well have thousands of review sites on one hosting account.

If you do not want to create product review sites, there are alternatives. Some affiliate sites offer you pre-made products and websites and are available for free for your use if you join their affiliate program.

Promoting Your Product

The seller in essence does all the conversion work; you just have to send targeted traffic to the sales page.

1.Blogging

This involves creating a blog, either specifically for the offers you are promoting or for a more general topic that is closely related with the offers.

For example, if you intend to promote electric blenders for 123 Electronics using a blog, your blog can be focused on the specific model of blender you want to promote, on blenders of different brands, or even on kitchen appliances in general.

2. Forum marketing

This involves joining and participating actively in a forum where there are users who are likely to be interested in the products or services you are promoting.

Your goal would be to offer helpful information to others, while recommending your offers in a subtle way.

3. Social media marketing

You can also promote your merchant's offers on Facebook, Twitter, and other social media platforms. A smart way to achieve success with this strategy is to create a group or page that is catered to users who are very likely to be interested in the products or services you're promoting. Your aim here is to offer helpful information related to your merchant's offers and promoting those offers covertly.

4. Email marketing

This very popular strategy involves creating an incentive such as a free e-book or journals that will attract the attention of people who are likely to be interested in the products or services you are promoting, and then using that incentive as bait to get them to join your mailing list. After building a huge list of subscribers and maintaining a cordial relationship with them through helpful information, you can pitch them the products or services you are promoting.

Other strategies include ;

Article Marketing: Write an article describing the features and benefits of the product.

eMail Marketing: Use your article as an advertisement in mailing lists.

Classified Ads: These are available all over the Internet for free.

Pay Per Click Marketing: Choose the best place for your ads.

Regardless of the platform you choose, your ultimate goal is to make money by encouraging people to buy whatever you are promoting by visiting the merchant's online store through your unique affiliate link.

Many of the larger affiliate sites offer training and promotional materials for your use for free.You are only limited by your imagination on how to market your affiliate link. Be creative. Step "outside the box" and create a new way that works for you. You can also research Online Marketing by searching the Internet. Online Marketing is a huge field and there are tons of informational products already written on the subject. Take advantage of that and you are on your way to financial freedom.

SOME NOTABLES KEYWORDS ON AFFILIATE MARKETING

Also referred to as performance marketing, affiliate marketing is a form of performance-based advertising in which a business pays its affiliates based on the actions of a visitor or customer brought to the business through the affiliate's own marketing efforts. Brands and agencies offer affiliate opportunities to publishers while affiliates sign up to market for advertisers. Below are some of the terms or definitions in the affiliate word.

- **Advertiser**

Often referred to as the merchant, the advertiser is either the company that produces the products or services affiliates promote or the company that brand hired to advertiser for them. Advertisers pay affiliates or networks for delivering traffic that generates a sale or lead for their brand.

- **Affiliate**

An individual (or company) who promotes products or services for a merchant in exchange for commission based off the sales and leads acquired. Affiliates are also known as **publishers.**

- *Affiliate Manager*

The person who manages an affiliate program for a merchant. They are responsible for recruiting publishers, policing affiliate activity and increasing overall sales for the advertiser. An affiliate manager acts as liaison between the affiliate and the merchant; they may work in-house for the advertiser or be an independent service provider contracted run their affiliate program.

- *Affiliate Network*

A third-party company that provides affiliate program management services for multiple brands. Affiliate networks have their own pool of affiliates for which they provide the tracking technology to report clicks, sales and leads. They allow advertisers opportunities for more exposure assuming their network includes reputable publishers with quality traffic.

- ***Click-Through-Rate (CTR)***

Clicking through refers to the act of someone clicking on an affiliate link and being taken to the merchant's website. Click-through-rate is a percentage rate that measures the number of times an affiliate link has been clicked on divided the number of times the link has been viewed. That number is then multiplied by 100 to find the percentage rate.

- ***Conversion Rate***

Conversions are actions successfully completed by a visitor or customer based on the pre-defined point of sale established between advertiser and affiliate. The action could be a click, a credit card submission during a sale, or signing up for an email list. Conversion rates show the number of times your affiliate link has generated a predefined conversion compared to the number of times the link has been viewed displayed as a percentage. Similar to the CTR, conversion rates are calculated by diving the amount of sales a link has generated by the number of impressions the link received and multiplying the result by 100.

- **Cookies**

A cookie is a small file that is added to a browser by a site or redirector domain, allowing the site to recognize the user when he or she returns. Specific to affiliate marketing, cookies are used as a tracking alternate to pixels. They assign an ID to a user that has clicked on an affiliate link to get to a merchant website for a predefined period. If that user completes a conversion, the affiliate is credited for the sale based off the cookie recognition, regardless of whether or not they completed the sale using the affiliate link on a repeat visit.

- *Cost Per Action (CPA)*

Cost Per Action, or Cost Per Acquisition, refers to the amount of money paid to obtain a desired outcome such as a completed sale or signup.

- ***Cost Per Click (CPC)***

Cost Per Click refers to the amount of money paid to generate a click by a user on an affiliate link. This is calculate by the number of clicks generated divided by the total campaign cost.

- ***Cost Per Thousand (CPM)***

Cost Per Thousand refers to the amount of money it costs to display an advertisement per 1000 impressions.

- **Creative**

A type of graphical ad or text link provided to the affiliate for use in promoting the affiliate program.

- ***Earnings Per Click (EPC)***

Earnings Per Click is the average amount earned every time someone clicks on an affiliate link. To find EPC, divide the amount generated in commissions from an affiliate link and by the total number of clicks that link received. If a campaign generates $3000 through an affiliate link and that that link received 8,000 clicks, the EPC would be $.38.

- ***Insertion Order***

Insertion orders outline campaign details in addition to the terms and conditions agreement that advertisers and affiliates sign prior to commencing their working relationship. IOs enforce affiliate compliance, specify payout amounts per conversion, define traffic sources allowed and dictate campaign duration.

- ***Outsourced Program Manager (OPM)***

Outsourced Program Managers are third-party account representatives who work independently of an advertiser to find affiliates and ensure campaign success. OPMs are also considered affiliate managers and provide the services an advertiser needs to be profitable through affiliate marketing without having to take on the expense in- house.

- **Pixel**

Pixels are HTML codes programmed onto a confirmation page that report sales when a conversion has occurred.There are four main types of pixels: javascript, iframe, image, and postback (or servertoserver). Each of these pixels is designed to pass customer information back to an advertiser or network based on a successful conversion so that commissions can be paid out accordingly.

- *Tracking Link*

Advertisers provide tracking links to each of their affiliates or networks that includes a unique code specifically assigned to that account. Using this link, advertisers and networks can track the number of conversions acquired by a specific affiliate, allowing them to gauge performance.

- *Unique Click*

Unique clicks track the number of original (or unique) visitors have clicked on an affiliate link versus seeing the total number of clicks (raw clicks) that have occurred. If someone clicks on an affiliate link 3 times, only one click would be counted. Unique clicks have a cookie persistence of 24 hours so if the same user came back more than a day later and re-clicked the affiliate link, another unique click would track, making it a total of 2 unique clicks and 4 raw clicks for that user.

- **White Label**

White labeling refers to a merchant allowing an affiliate to sell products under their own brand with no mention of the actual merchant. The advertisements are designed uniquely for the affiliate pushing the offer and often make no mention of the outside merchant.This can improve the conversion rate by convincing consumers that the product or service is solely available from the publisher. Most advertisers merchants limit white labeling opportunities to their top-performing and most trusted affiliates.

If you want to be successful at affiliate marketing avoid filling up every page of your site with tons of banners. If banner ads were the key to affiliate marketing success, everyone would be a millionaire. A site loaded with banner on top of banner looks very ugly and does not make visitors want to click on the ad.

When looking to increase the money you make from affiliate marketing, diversification of the products that you sell is a great suggestion. If you can find a particular niche that you can select products from and focus your marketing towards that niche, then large amounts of sales could be on the horizon. Reaching out to these niche markets can be just what you need for affiliate marketing success.

Affiliate marketing success depends on building traffic to your affiliate web site or blog. One way to build traffic is to create videos and post them on the popular video sites online. They can be how-to videos or product reviews. Make your videos upbeat, entertaining and honest and viewers will respond by checking out your site, clicking through to your affiliate and likely making a purchase.

The key to affiliate marketing success is trying out everything once, and then trying it again later. For example, if a certain affiliate is not successful for you now, try a different tactic with it in a month. It does not hurt you to try and you never know what might be successful in the future.

So, after reading and applying the helpful tips listed above, you should feel a bit more at ease in the land of affiliate marketing. You have the tools and now it is time to use them. You should feel empowered and ready to begin your affiliate marketing journey to better promote your business and make larger profits.

- ***Signing Up For Every Program Related To Your Niche***

Many affiliates sign up for every program under the sun related to their niche. While it is a good idea to promote two or three products or services that you believe would be useful or valuable to your readers, it is not a good idea to promote 5,7 or even more products. When you go overboard, your visitors will notice that your site seems to be overly promotional - and the search engines will, too.

Focus on valuable content, and promote a few quality products gently. Try to choose offers that are best suited to the needs of your readers. And remember, you are not "stuck" with the products you choose - you should test to see which products have higher conversion rates.

- ***Promoting Products That Are Not Relevant To Your Website***

119

Search engines pay attention to the relevancy between your niche, content, and the products or services you offer - and so do your visitors. You do not want to send a mixed message, or confuse your visitors. If your niche is dog training, you absolutely do not want content on your site (or banners, ads, etc.) promoting breast enhancement pills! Your readers may be offended, and it will absolutely take away from your credibility.Stick to content that your readers want, that is on topic. Choose credible affiliate programs that are relevant to your niche.

- *Throwing Advertising Rules Out The Window*

We have all seen banner ads, email messages and other advertising that make huge (and unbelievable) promises. A buying customer does not usually realize that you are an affiliate; they look at you as the merchant, and trust that you offer reputable products. As an affiliate, think about the banners and other forms of advertising the merchant offers before you begin using them. If it sounds like a bunch of "hype" that you may not be able to live up to, think twice before using that advertising medium. Never make unsubstantiated claims, as it may come back to "bite" you in the form of dissatisfied customers - and potential legal problems.

To avoid this pitfall, simply make sure that the language used in advertising the product is ethical, and avoid overselling. When writing product reviews, as many affiliates do, be honest and transparent - and never steal content from the vendor's original product site to use in your review. It may be against policy, and Google may see it as duplicate content as well.

- ### *Failing To Commit Sufficient Time Or Resources To Affiliate Campaigns*

No matter how much you wish it were true, you cannot throw up an affiliate site, put some content on it, links to products, banners, etc. and expect to make money. Successful affiliate marketing requires sufficient time, money, or both. The more affiliate campaigns you run, the more resources are required. In order to reach a certain level of success, you have got to promote and market your product which can be done through article syndication, list building, social media, forums, blogging, pay-per-click ads and more.

How can you avoid this pitfall? Know how much you can do depending on your lifestyle, job, kids, etc. If you need an hour each day for each affiliate campaign, dedicate "x" number of hours per day according to how many campaigns you are running. If you do not have the time to manage promotions and marketing yourself, outsource the work.

- ***Unrealistic Expectations - Or, Abandoning Ship Too Quickly***

You cannot become an overnight success in affiliate marketing, although we had all love it if it was possible! So many marketers build a website and begin affiliate marketing, only to abandon ship when they do not see results in a week or two. This is not how it works, especially considering the sheer volume of competition in most markets today. Building successful affiliate marketing campaigns takes time and patience.

Quick fix? Set realistic goals, and make them small ones. Say you want to make $50 per week, and grow to where you are earning $60 per week within a 7 week time span.

Email Marketing has rapidly become one of the most powerful tools in global business history. Responsible email Marketing which is distinct from spamming or sending of bulk messages has a unique style of its own. Here are some of the tips for a beginner in the affiliate business;

- ### *3% of Affiliate Marketers Exposed*

Proven statistics show that only 3% of Affiliate Marketers use the opt-in list building strategy for making follow-ups with potential clients out of the 110,000 + Clickbank Affiliates. Now if you are not building an opt-in list, you will not see one cent or shilling as the case maybe.

Super Affiliate Marketers know this rule and that is why they consistently make a six-figure annual income using follow-ups for their eMail Marketing campaigns. So get set to first of all set up an autoresponder account with Getresponse, AWeber or other good ones that suit your personal style and budget and have a blast.

- ***Generate Highly-Targeted Traffic***

Advertise your autoresponders and squeeze pages specially set up to collect your potential subscriber's email addresses on targeted high-traffic sites. If you have no traffic - No targeted high-traffic coming into your affiliate Web sites, then you will become a sitting duck. So, advertise using paid advertising by placing well crafted classified ads with subcriber bases of 1500 to over 100,000 if you can find good publications and Google AdWords starting with $5 - and depending on the keywords you bid on.

- ***Offer A Valuable Item To Download***

To collect emails you have to offer something of perceived value to your potential clients. If it is not exclusive or original - like a newletter publication, an eBook on traffic generation or a free software download -but a rehashed and beaten-to-death item with a less than $20 value - in my opinion, then do not offer it or else the highly-targeted traffic of unique visitors to your niche blog or Web site will not be motivated to subscribe to your free stuff or even return regularly to your site.

- ***Time-Specific Follow-Ups***

Now, after setting up your autoresponder accounts, you need to cut and paste the affiliate program's sales letters, solo ads, text links etc., within the autoresponder messages area. These follow-ups can be made up to 7 times or more on auto pilot that is you just have to select the dates and times to send your messages from anywhere you are in the world. You could be on a business travel to Singapore or a pleasure and holiday trip to the Caribbean island of Barbados and still have money flooding your bank accounts.

Now, very regular follow-up messages can make it seem like you are being too pushy or using hard tactics to market your products and services in front of potential clients or subscribers and they will simply unsuscribe before you even utter the word - "Affiliate!" It is far better to send out each message over 2 or 3-Day intervals or whatever interval you decide to use and all will be well.

- ***Tracking And Testing Of Your Campaigns***

It is also very important to know the source of your customer traffic so that you can get rid off those that are not profitable and concentrate on those that work. For example, if you advertise with your classified ads, you may wish to track the click-through and sales conversion rates of each ad campaign.

Like it is stated above, getting to give away a valuable free item should also be uppermost in your mind so that you can make those follow-ups which will lead to eventual sales!

Summarily,following these quick email marketing tips for affiliate marketers responsibly will enable you to literally skyrocket your online income in record time while building a mailing list of highly-targeted and responsive audience from around the world who you can sell to again and again.

AUTORESPONDER

E-mail marketing campaigns can often be make-or-break propositions for Internet marketers. One of the affiliate marketing secrets that can stack the deck in your favor is choosing the best autoresponder review for your business. A quality autoresponder review can help you sift through all the details and narrow down your choices.

Autoresponders are software programs. The software can be embedded in a website. It can function as a kind of secretary by answering emails.

The first companies to use autoresponders were big companies. As the technology has improved and the years have gone by, the software has become less expensive.

It is a perfect tool for the small business owner. Big companies can afford to hire more employees. Small businesses need to think "outside the box" in order to avoid hiring more employees.

The first use of autoresponder software was to reply to customer emails. The software became more common as e-businesses became more popular.

The programs can work in a variety of ways. One simple pattern is initiated when the customer places an order. An automatically generated email is sent to the customer, usually with a "no-reply", as the email address is not monitored. The autoresponders used in the affiliate marketing business are different.

When a new visitor reaches your website, several things can happen. You can have a pop-up window announcing a free e-book for any visitor providing a valid email address.

You could even include a line saying that the offer is for a limited time only, encouraging people to "hurry". When the visitor signs up, your software will automatically send the e-book to the email address provided.

In the e-book, you will include a number of links to relevant websites. The books usually include more information about the products you are promoting.

The autoresponder program can be used in another way for affiliate marketing. You can offer all of your website visitors a free newsletter. All they need to do is provide a first name and a valid email address.

There are newsletters about pets, health, herbs, kids, clothing, shopping and travel, just to name a few. Practically every subject could be reported about in a regular newsletter.

If the information you provide is valuable, your readers will enjoy it and they will be more likely to buy the products you recommend. Ultimately, that is how an autoresponder makes money for your business. But there is one more advantage.

Every email address captured by the program can be used for future campaigns. You might promote similar products in the future.

Your database can be used to keep a detailed list of "who" signed up for "which" newsletter at "what" website. That is how an autoresponder and the right database design can help you grow your affiliate marketing business.

What Is An Autoresponder?

An autoresponder is an email management system that allows you to pre-schedule email responses to your subscribers. When a new subscriber signs up to your list, the autoresponder kicks into action and starts the marketing process with your new list member. From this point on, presuming you have preloaded your campaign emails, the autoresponder does your marketing for you. You just sit back and wait for the responses.

How Do I Set Up An Autoresponder?

1) *Sign up for an account* with one of the many autoresponder companies out there. A few to consider are:

Aweber

Mailchimp

Get Response

Constant Contact

2) *Load your campaign with your email promotions.* Start with the first email, then add your follow-up emails. Do not forget to set up a ***Thank You*** email as your first response. Be sure to schedule your emails a reasonable number of days apart from each other. Start with spacing them just a day or two apart, then slow down to once a week as the campaign goes on. Expect to get a certain amount of unsubscribers in the beginning. This is normal, and nothing to worry about. A small, high quality list is better than a large, low quality one.

Some Tips

> ➤ Add your email address to the campaign so you can see what your customers are getting.

➢ Make sure all of the links in your emails work. If you have eBook downloads, be sure they actually can be downloaded.
➢ Regularly check your autoresponder to make sure all of the information is up-to-date, and to insert any new promotions.

In summary, do not try to do an affiliate marketing campaign without an autoresponder. Try a few to see which one is the most user-friendly for your purposes. Most offer free, or low-cost trial periods.

How a good autoresponder works?

A good autoresponder review will fill you in on what good autoresponder services do. The very best autoresponders, do the following:

- *Provide A Good Delivery Rate.*

Delivery rate is essentially the percentage of your emails that get to your prospective clients. Getting your e-mails through the spam and junk mail gates are imperative to the success of your marketing efforts.

- ***Handle List Management And Analysis.***

A good autoresponder will help you collect and process information about the effectiveness of your efforts. Internet marketers should be able to review their subscribers, read any messages they may have been sent and analyze clicks and historical page open rates to further refine their efforts.

One of the key affiliate marketing secrets is auto responder delivery rates. A good autoresponder provides good delivery rates and is easy to use for list management and analysis purposes, you are in good shape.

The following is a review of three of the top autoresponders

Using Aweber correctly is one of the easiest affiliate marketing secrets to master. Aweber is a simple to use program that allows marketers to quickly and easily insert audio or video into their pages and manage subscribers, even substantial lists of them.

It is easy to schedule and sequence using Aweber, and the program is very straightforward and intuitive. Aweber also offers a very useful tracking function that allows you to keep track of how successful your efforts are.

> ➢ **Autoresponse Plus**

Autoresponse Plus is another great program. If you are looking for quality affiliate marketing secrets, you need to learn the ins and outs of this program. You pay a one-time fee for the use of this program, but it is money well spent. You will need someone with extensive tech knowledge to tutor you to get the full use of this program, however.

> **Get Response**

Get response is another great affiliate marketing secrets to success. This is an industry leading program that stacks up well to Aweber. It is easy to use, customizable and allows for a great range of uses. The versatility of this program is a great selling point. You can use it for just about any purpose, and the program is very compatible with many sources of content, including text and video providers. Also, it provides fantastic analytic tools. It is a little cheaper than Aweber, but does have a monthly fee.

Finding a good autoresponder is one of the key affiliate marketing secrets to success. Get it right, and you are well on your way to success. Do not be afraid to spend a little money to get the best from your autoresponder.

The affiliate marketing business model is like being a commission paid sales person. There are lots of different products and services that you can promote as an affiliate. They start from low priced items where you can usually earn around $10 commission per sale all the way up to high ticket affiliate programs where you can earn in excess of $1000 commission per sale.

Here Are Strategiess To Mastering High Ticket Affiliate Programs.

- *Know Why People Will Want The Product or Service.*

People buy high priced items because they provide an exceptional difference and value as compared to a lower priced product. Just think of air travel. If a first class airline ticket did not offer anything different to a regular economy airline ticket, people would not travel first class. The people who buy high priced items are willing to pay a lot more if they get many more benefits and advantages that a low priced item offers.

- ***People Want Solutions.***

We are all continually looking for answers to our problems and ways to make our life easier and more comfortable. Lower cost products may do part of the job but often do not always provide all the tools and resources that we may need to reach our objective in the manner and timescale that we want. There are high ticket affiliate programs in most markets where people are willing to pay more to reach their objectives quicker and more effectively.

- ***Believe In Your Products.***

In the affiliate marketing business some affiliates will sell any product to any person. If you want to get involved with high ticket affiliate programs you have to be passionate about the product you are selling and truly believe that it does deliver value.

- ### *The Numbers Make Sense.*

Low cost products can be much easier to sell but you have to sell a lot to make a realistic income. Suppose you want to make $4000 per month and you were selling a product that paid you $40 commission per sale. You would have to sell 100 products and that is not easy, especially if you have only just started or you have a small customer list. But if you are selling a product that pays you $2000 commission, you would only have to sell two to achieve your objective.

- ### *Have A Proven Marketing Funnel.*

It is very unlikely that a customer will buy a high ticket item from you the first time that they visit your website or sales pages. So you have to build a relationship with them using proven marketing funnel. This is the process that starts from the time when a prospective customer clicks on your link to them becoming a customer who wants to buy from you.

HIGH TICKET MARKETING *– Highly Profitable!*

Here are quick and easy ways you can use to boost your selling power with high ticket affiliate marketing.

- ***Stand Out Different From Your Competition. Setup Your USP.***

It is extremely important that you differentiate yourself from your competitors to make sure that you sell your high profit products. If you provide the same old information that your competitors have been selling then there will be no difference between you and them. You have to lay out one super powerful benefit that makes you absolutely different and why people should consider purchasing your product.

- ***How To Break Even Your Advertising Expenses And Test Your High Priced Product Conversion?***

It is very important that you break even your advertising expense almost instantly as soon as you promote your high priced product. The best thing you can do is setup a one time offer page on your site where you provide a low cost product offer that is displayed to your visitor as soon as he subscribes to your list. This will make sure that this product sells on continuous basis and this will give you more money to continuously drive traffic to your site. Make sure you get started small.

- ***Start A Small Campaign And Roll Out Big.***

It is important that you start small and test your campaign before you spend lots of money promoting your campaign. Starting small is important because once you are driving profits you can then take it to the big level and this will help you to play a somewhat risk free game.

- ***Sales Funnel Secrets To Explosive Profits.***

Make sure that you setup a simple sales funnel where you promote your high cost product along with low cost products and few affiliate products. Having all such combination in place will help you to keep making money from low cost products and make big money out of your high cost products.

- ***4 Places To Put Your High End Product Offer To Explode Your Sales.***

These are the four places to get started;

1. On your one time offer page when subscribers signs in to your list.

2. On your thank you page.

3. In your confirmation page when the subscriber confirms his subscription.

4. On the order page as an upsell when the subscriber purchases one of your other products.

Please note these;

- ✓ A high ticket product is any product or service that sells for more than $500 or

$1000.

- ✓ An Affiliate is someone who sells other people's products.

- • *Perks, Perks, Perks*

You often get other types of perks or fringe benefits on high ticket products besides your percentage of the sale.

Let us take seminar or workshop seat sales as an example. As a seminar affiliate, your job is to "put butts in seats". So, if a seminar ticket costs $3997 and your affiliate fee is $1000 per seat, you sell 4 seats and you make $4000. Not bad! But, in many cases, the seminar promoter also offers a deal where if you sell so many seats, you can go to the seminar for free! They might run a "Sell 2, Go for Free" campaign. So, not only do you make $4000 but you get to attend the $3997 seminar for free and sometimes the seminar promoter will offer an additional cut of the sales if you sell over a minimum number of seats to their event. So, if you sell over 8 seats, you might get an additional $400 for every seat over 8 you sell. Even if this is not offered, you can often negotiate a deal like this with the promoter. These are just a few examples. There are many other types of perks that are available or that you can negotiate.

- ***Super Affiliate Extras***

Supposing you are very good at affiliate selling high ticket products. You could become known as a super affiliate. A super affiliate is simply an affiliate who is capable of generating a significant percentage of the sales of any affiliate program. In other words, you are "kicking butt" and producing more sales and revenue than many if not all of the other affiliates in a product owners affiliate program. Now, most product owners, if they are smart, know that it is vital for them to recognize and reward these super affiliates. After all, they are selling more product then anybody else and they want to encourage them to continue to do so.So many product owners will give a higher percentage of product sales to super affiliates. If normal affiliates receive 40% of each sale, super affiliates might get 55% to 65%.

Super affiliates may also be given advance opportunity to sell new products being introduced by a product marketer. This means they get to sell the new product before all the other affiliates are allowed access to it plus, if you are the super affiliate, you can often negotiate other benefits, tailored specifically to what you want for selling these high ticket products.

- ***Multiple Streams of Income***

As an affiliate, you can help market multiple high ticket products. These products can come from the same or different product owners. And the products can be focused at the same or different target markets. So even if one product has a slow down in sales, the other products may be doing fine.

Now, I am not telling you to go out and become an affiliate for a ton of different high ticket products. You still need to choose products you believe in and that are of high quality. In the long term, this will serve you much better than a "scatter-gun" approach to high ticket affiliate sales.

But, the ability to chose several high quality high ticket items to market as an affiliate, means that you can diversify your income streams so that you are not dependent on one stream alone should the market slow in that area. Robert Allen calls this Multiple Streams of Income.It is just a sound business concept that you should follow, even as an affiliate!

- ***Differentiate or Die!***

There are a ton of products and product owners out there running affiliate programs. Many of these programs are marketing or selling E-Books or other low profit items. How will you differentiate yourself from all the other affiliates flogging the same low ticket products? I believe that the best way to set yourself apart from others is to sell high ticket products as an affiliate. Many existing affiliates are uncomfortable selling items with a big price tag because they have a hard time justifying the value of the product to themselves.This is why it is so important to sell only items you believe in. Your belief in a product comes from you having carefully evaluated the product and ensuring its high quality, yourself. But once you understand the benefits a product can provide, it is very easy to sell the product to others, even when it costs a lot more.And selling high ticket products gains you the appreciation and respect of product providers much more quickly than selling their low ticket items will. That appreciation can translate into the perks and extras we have mentioned earlier.

High ticket affiliate selling puts you in another class from those who only do affiliate sales of low ticket items!

• *Continuous Residual Income*

Another type of high ticket item is the product or service that has not a fixed amount, one time sale. Instead, the customer purchases a product or service where they continue to make regular payments.

Examples of this type of high ticket item are membership sites, shopping cart service or monthly hosting fees.

Many affiliate programs are setup such that you continue to receive a percentage or a fixed amount per period (e.g. monthly) as long as the person you sold the original membership remains a member of that service.

• *Multiple Tiers Means More Profit For You With No More Work!*

Some affiliate programs are also setup such that you can also make money from 2nd tier sales.

2nd tier sales are simply any sales of a product that a customer buys from the same product owner or marketer after the first one that you sell that customer as an affiliate.

For example.

Supposing you sell an internet market marketing home study system for $1299 as an affiliate to Customer A. You get 50% of the sale or $649.50.

Customer A is very happy with the product and decides to buy the advanced internet marketing home study system directly from the creator of the original home study system for $2299.

Now, you were not involved in the 2nd sale at all. But because the affiliate system you joined was of the 2 tier variety, your agreement with that affiliate program says that you get 25% of all future sales of any products in the affiliate program to the same customer you original brought in for the first sale.

So because Customer A is buying another product within the same affiliate program and he was originally sold his first product by you.You get 25% of that sale or $574.75.

LOW AND HIGH-TICKET AFFILIATE PRODUCTS -*The difference!*

Affiliate marketing has really come along way from where it was just some years ago, and we have the internet to thank for that. Many exciting opportunities and avenues have been opened up, with new niche markets being discovered all the time. As affiliates, it is our job to tap these resources and earn as much money as possible for ourselves and our families through free affiliate opportunities.

You may have seen those nifty $5 products floating around the internet. Have you ever bought one of them? Did you find it useful? Would you buy another one from the same owner? Chances are you would answer yes to these questions. Most of the time these products offer a lot of good value and prove to be useful.

Would you promote any of these products? If they provide value and offer help to their specific market, then of course you would, right? But, think about this then, how much money could you expect to make promoting $5 products as an affiliate?

I am sure that has you are thinking now think about those $2,000 or higher products, tele-seminars, webinars, classes, etc. that people sign up for all the time. Did you know you can be an affiliate for those as well? There are numerous free affiliate opportunities for high-ticket items on the internet.

I bet you are thinking about how much more money you could make by selling just one of those products. You are right; you can make a lot more money just in one affiliate commission. But here is the catch. As an affiliate marketer, if you are just starting out, you want to be promoting the low-ticket items.

Why? For one, it will be easier to make the sale, especially if you are new to affiliate marketing. But, it also helps build trust and will have your customers coming back to you for more recommendations. What do you recommend to them next time? Maybe not a $1,000 price tag, but eventually it can lead to that.

Above all, start out small with low-ticket free affiliate opportunities, and then promote high-ticket products on the back-end once you have gained trust among your website visitors, newsletter subscribers, blog readers, etc.

CONCLUSION

We may conclude that choosing an affiliate program that is right for you might be time consuming but a worth while process. Going through the above whole process will also be a learning curve for new entrepreneurs who are serious about starting a successful home based business. So there is an opportunity for business students and young entrepreneur to develop a simple website with limited budget that can be arranged easily through their own personal savings.

Just remember, if you keep doing what you are doing now, you can expect to keep getting the same results. We urge you to challenge yourself, move off your comfort zone and try something new. It can be very rewarding both in satisfaction and financially.

You do not have to wait to become a full time marketer to enjoy affiliate marketing. Use it for a little extra christmas money or to put a little spending money in your pocket you can just blow on something you have been waiting for.

30325400R00090

Printed in Great
Britain
by Amazon